Spiritual Doors

Lavance Washington

The Reading Glass Books
1-888-420-3050
www.readingglassbooks.com
production@readingglassbooks.com

Contents

Dedicated to the Holy Spirit

Acknowledgments

Since I have been saved and called to write this book, the Holy Spirit has and still does play a tremendous part in my life through communication, reading my Bible, and praying for others while encouraging them also.

There is no way I can have a commitment so great without God in my life, so first and foremost, I would like to acknowledge the God in me. I also dedicate this book to Jesus Christ, my Lord and Savior, who have kept me through the episodes of my life of growth and the pursuit of wholeness.

I acknowledge my grandmother, Earle L. Ancar, who prayed for me her entire life. She opened the door for me to live. As a matter of fact, she keeps the doors open. I'm grateful to her for allowing this door to open for me so I can begin to write this book God had given me to write.

My grandmother lives in San Francisco, where she has been living since 1950. Her intentions for this house is that no one in her family will ever become homeless. It has been an open door for the saints who need a safe place to stay, and now it is a door front for me to complete the assignment God has given me inside this book.

Last but never least, I must acknowledge this house and all the doors that are connected to it. There are twenty-seven doors inside this three-bedroom, three-story house, and every one of them plays a significant role. There have been plenty of roles, family roles as I beginner the role of growing up. I can remember the different outlooks of these many doors, and all of them are spiritual, from the front door to the last door, which is on the last floor. You will have an opportunity to read about every one of these doors as I set aside a whole chapter later in this book just for them doors.

I want to acknowledge Nolia Rembert, a servant and much more, a true worshiper of Jesus Christ, the author of *Empty Sounds: God's Glory Devine Devotion's* for all her many other accomplishments in just being a good spiritual writer. She was able to help me bring all this together as I told my story to her at my grandmother's house, she diligently worked on my story, and I truly thank her and pray that God will show favor in every area of her life.

The last part of this book will be demonic words from your own mouth.

Lavance Washington, at the age of ten years old in school, remembers being slower than other students, unknowingly allowing low self- esteem to step in. At that age, the teachers did not make a big fuss over low self-esteem, using slow or just needing a special aid teacher for extra help.

The teachers planted seeds in Lavance's life by asking him plenty of questions like, "What's your favorite song?" At that time, sitting on the dock of the bay, watching the tides just roll away, not understanding the eras of time or even knowing that God had a plan for his life, Lavance swore by the song, not just allowing it to be his favorite song but also promising to live the life of it.

Sports was a plus as well as a favorite of his. He competed against teachers in basketball, balancing his life out to the best of his ability. It wasn't a big deal not knowing about his learning disability. Lavance did not feel alone with the teachers, but equal. That caused the balance of his learning disability simply because he felt alone a whole lot of times growing up as a child being born to a young mother and having a lonely spirit.

I found out later that the loneliness was an empty hole that was being delayed for the use of the Holy Spirit. Jerimiah 29:11 (NIV) says, I know the plans that I have for you, announces the Lord. I want you to enjoy success. I do not plan to harm you. I will give you hope."

Elementary school was fun for him, mostly because of the outside sports that took place then. Having a young mother didn't help with the search of love and the need to be equal with the rest of his peers. Being five feet five helped a lot. It also made him feel like a giant; it made him feel like he belonged and was good at something. He compared his height to the teachers who were the same height with him caused his learning disability to balance itself out with what he was good at. These are the things that helped him grow into the godly man he is today. It was different for him in the classroom. His performance was evasive, never being able to answer any of the teacher's questions.

Now I'm in junior high school, nothing really changed, except the fact that I started to go to church. My mother always told us about church and how much God loved us, but she never forced us to go, me and my siblings; there were five of us. There was a church bus that would come every Sunday. I was the only one that would get on the bus and go. I really didn't know why I liked going to church so much then. I didn't even know what it was all about or what the pastor was talking about. All I knew was I just liked the songs they sang. Then I stopped going. I don't believe I went a whole year.

It was an apostolic church. As a child, I didn't know God was opening the door of my life every time I got on that bus and went to that church. Seeds were being planted in that lonely place.

These were my junior high school years. The only classes I really enjoyed was math and PE. I became athlete of the year. To become the athlete of the year, you must be builder up. My building was through every sport inside the school I was attending. I was in the eighth grade playing basketball, football, wrestling, soccer, track and field, and was voted athlete of the year. I also won the state in wrestling. You can tell I love sports. I started playing football at an early age. I started with the police athlete league program, where they supported the youth in the neighborhood who were less fortunate all the way to high school. I grew up to be one of the best running backs in all the high schools.

I was transformed to another high school where I continued to play football with professionals, Mervyn Fernandez and Jim McMahon, who I grew up with and became friends with. They became professional football players with the Oakland Raiders, and the other one with the Chicago Bears. I also started my first job at the car wash while the record "Car Wash" came out. We had a lot of fun there. We had a bebop music box. Listening to the music made my job easier and fun. I met all kinds of people, including my first wife. I was still living inside my mother and stepfather's house, saving up my money so I could get an apartment for me and my lady. My stepfather knew I was working, and because we were staying with him, he wanted me to pay him rent even though I was still a teenager and even though I needed to save money for me and my girl to move. My stepfather was often upset because my mother supported me and allowed me to rest on the weekends before my baseball games while my brother was doing yard work. My stepfather didn't like that. He thought I need to do yard work also. I would hear him and my mother argue all the time. I did recognize the spirit of greed on him. He even pulled a gun on me, and instantly I knew it was time for me to go. Suddenly, a door of hatred opened. I began to hate him. It's not like I ever liked him because he never played a role in my life in the first place.

I did get an apartment in San Jose, California, but never changed my address from my mother and stepfather's house. I was young, and there were some things I just wasn't attending to, such as life matters, which includes changing addresses and other matters that come when getting on with life. I went to a baseball trading camp for the San Francisco Giants in Santa Clara, California. This is when things start to get a little tough. All the mail the Giants was sending to me went to my parents' house. I never got that mail because my stepfather was so evil. He was angry because I didn't give in to his desires for my life when he never cared anyway. He tore up every letter that had my name on it. He was determined to pray against me instead of praying for me or living life as an example for me. I don't know what was in them letters; it could have been another door of success for me. It was seven years later that God convicted him and had him to confess.

Yeah, it was painful for me, and today I thank God that I am healed and set free from that door he opened for me to have a bitter spirit. God made me better.

Romans 8:28 says all things work together for the good in them who were called for his purpose.

His mom had to work to support her family alone, with his father working at a store called Gymco. Then eventually he got a job working at Safeway store as a janitor. Him and his father never really talked. He was doing his thing, and Lavance was doing his. His mom working all the time caused him to lean onto his teachers for the affection and development he needed at that time

My mother passed in August 27, 2012. I also lost my oldest brother just one year before her death.

It was the grieving process of losing my family members that caused the change that has taken place in my life.

Prison Doors

After I moved in with my first wife, I bought me a van. I began to hang out with the wrong crowds, which was the first door to the prison systems opening up for me. I call them so-called friends for the simple fact that when they would do bad things, such as burglaries or that sort of negative activities, they will call me to pick them up alone with stolen property.

They will have me take stolen property to an undercover police officer. He was buying stolen goods for cash. Later on, I found out it is was a sting operation. Eventually, I got arrested along with them. I ended up in jail under all kinds of trumped-up charges. Murder was one of them. They eventually sent me to Vacaville Prison for a ninety-day observation. Once it was over, I ended up back in Santa Clara County Ranch for eighteen months, and I didn't commit one crime, but what I did find out was I was scared. I was scared of the public defender who had earned the name public pretender (through my own judgement). The public defender was trained to interrogate people into filling up the prison system. I was one of them people.

Pipe Doors

Once I returned home to San Jose, I began to work as a janitor for Lucky, a grocery store. I started hanging out with my friend who was working at Lucky Store also. He was the one who got me the job.

Also, I trusted this guy because at the time I was selling cocaine, and I was his supplier. I had the highest respect for him. He turned me on to powder cocaine. He didn't know I had been smoking marijuana too. The actual gateway to hard-core drugs such as cocaine and heroin, and now even crystal meth. He came over to cop from me one night. He tried to convince me on several occasions to try smoking the cocaine he cooked up over at my house.

One particular night, he came over, and he had already known I had a weakness with ladies and drugs together. This was one of those night he was able to convince me to hit the pipe through a female tale. He said to me the mixture of a woman and crack cocaine was the best it came, and that was the bait. He was right. When I blew that smoke out, I blew the door to my addiction wide open and ended up in places I never wanted to see. He taught me how to cook up drugs. It had become a nonstop roller coaster as I became more and more addicted to the crack cocaine. I would inhale daily, looking for that first hit that I took. All the others after that was similar but never like the first one.

My First Door Encounter with Satan

My first encounter with spiritual doors happened on a Sunday. I lived in San Jose with a girlfriend. We lived inside an apartment complex. We were both using crack cocaine at the time. I believe it was obvious that we were on crack. There also was a minister who stayed there too. This is one of the main reasons I believe the minister who lived inside the same apartment complex we lived in always invited us to church. Every time we saw him, he would always ask us when we were coming to church with him, so finally we decided to accept his invitation to go to church on a Sunday. The minister dropped us off at home when the services was over with.

And right after getting back home, we were walking a distance to the front door of our house, which was approximately 30 yards away. As we both approached, I noticed something at the door. It looked like the devil. I turned to look at my girlfriend and asked if she saw the same thing. She said yes, it looked like the devil dressed in red, just for a split second.

The guy at the door was someone I knew but never kept company with. He caught us by surprise. He had an ounce of crack cocaine in his possession, wanting to get us high. This was the first time he ever approached us this way, and being that we were just coming from church, we were being tired already, but it was the first time I realized I had a spiritual eye for what the enemy was capable of doing. God revealed to us the attack of the enemy at our front door.

This was the beginning of my personal journey to Christ and the spiritual war of doors closing and opening.

"Bless be the Lord my Rock who trains my hands how to war" (Psalm 144:1).

Another door that was opened was a door that I opened myself, and this particular door I opened was also presented to me by the enemy, but I was not aware.

There are two types of doors and two ways of opening and closing these doors. One type is the God type, simply put, and the other is the doors Satan sends out assignments to open. (*Screwtape Letters* desribes it really well.)

This is also why God has given us the authority to cancel the assignments of the devil, and this should take place early in the mornings upon arising, the morning glory of crushing Satan's head under your feet then rebuking him so that you may live a life of freedom.

I'm not saying there will not be no more warfare 'cause that is what takes place as you enter into the kingdom of God. Satan is always trying to get us back into his kingdom, but he has to get permission from God to make it happen. God will not give him permission inside our lives if he knows we are not ready and able to conquer the enemy.

Then there are the doors that God opens in order for us to become developed into holiness, the doors God uses to get us to the places we need to be in him. And there are so many of those doors. God wants us to make it through every door he has for us to go through, and he also wants every door that he closes to be so tightly locked until we won't return. We have to get through these doors through his Word.

I allowed my friend to come in and live with me for three days. He offered me $1,000 with the money out in his hand in plain view. That was a boatload of money back then, especially to an addict. Of course, I said yes and took the money. Any addict can confess to money being a trigger.

That's exactly what it had become to me. I let him stay and was determined to know where and how he got that kind of money from, and I just needed him to turn me on so I could have some big money also.

I did not know at that time that "for the love of money is a root to all evil" (1 Tim. 6:10, NKJV). As I continued to converse with him about the money, I found out then that there are so many doors to life. This door was being opened by him because as I continued to converse with him, he opened up the door to me becoming a driver for the robberies that the money came from. Those robberies were jewelry robberies that I soon became addictive too.

After so many robberies and after having lots of money, my girl and myself—by this time, we had a daughter, she was a year old—left to Bridgeport, Connecticut, with a dream to live and try a new beginning because of the type of lifestyle I had developed. Besides, she had family there, and it was a perfect escape. We left everything behind except the jewelry, our clothes, and the money that I had already made from (I thought) an old lifestyle, excited about the new life we were to enter into. It never crossed my mind to invest my money in an area where it will continue to grow.

Anyone who is on drugs, they do not think intelligently. There is nothing positive about being an addict except where that next hit of drugs is going to come from, so allow me to take this time and insert the thoughts of you receiving Jesus Christ as Lord of your life.

Upon arriving to Connecticut, we moved into my girl's auntie's house. This house was so huge; it was three different floors, and to my surprise, there were so many demonic doors. Only, these doors were so heavy. I could feel the darkness that surrounded me inside the house.

There where so many grown people addicted to heroin coming in and out of these doors. These were not my doors but someone else's doors. I was very uncomfortable down in Connecticut. Heroin was the thing, but it was not my thing. My thing was crack still. My recovery was shady, with relapse being part of it, so here I am now going through other people's doors to get to my own door.

Back at the crack door, I found out my behavior was still there on repeat. I got extremely uncomfortable and moved out, found my own place, got me a job, and took my family away from such horrible scenes.

I moved into my own place with my girl and two-year-old daughter. It was a one-bedroom. I found a job in a warehouse, packing orders for customers. I did deliveries as well

Seem like everything was going well until one day, I came home, and her uncle told me that she wasn't being very nice when I was away and that she was doing bad things while I was away at work, so the uncle decided to meet me on my payday after my lunch break and give me a ride to the Greyhound bus station, where I bought a ticket to return back home to California. I didn't think her uncle was lying, so I went back to San Jose.

Once I arrived back in San Jose, California, my old behavior became my best friend again, and that was too bad for me. I started to rob jewelry stores again and this time was arrested by a police officer I grew up with. He pulled up right on the side of me at a stoplight at the same time I did. He knew right then and there who I was. He pulled me over, arrested me, and I ended up doing seven years in San Quentin Prison. Only this time, I was guilty.

Satanic Doors on Family through Bondage

On my arrival at San Quentin Prison, I was able to inform my sister of over $200,000 worth of diamonds hidden in her attic. I wanted her to sell some and give me some money. Her and my family took the diamonds and spent them all. They never sent me anything. I felt that door of hatred opening up more, and all I wanted to do was kill them all. I was so mad, especially my first year in San Quentin. I decided to go to church. I was scared. I was seeing people get stabbed and killed all day long. I still made a conscious decision to go. I had already accepted Jesus Christ at a younger age, so at San Quentin, I got baptized.

I was already singing in the San Quentin mass choir, but there was still hatred toward my family inside my spirit, causing me to be bitter and mad.

One night I went to bed to be awakened 3:00 a.m. by the Spirit of God. I was being lifted off my bed. I opened my eyes. God slammed me back on my bed. The very first thing that came out of my mouth was, "Thank you, Lord." He had already shown me in my mind how he was chastising me for the thoughts I had against my family. I could hear him clearly say, "Them diamonds was never yours from the start."

Freedom started approaching me in a way that only God can manifest. I felt every evil thought come from among my heart concerning my family. At that very moment, I realized I had been set free. I became humble.

Once I was released from prison, me and my wife got back together. Of course, coming out of prison, I couldn't find no job, so I started selling drugs again, and there it was, another demonic door coming in to do what it does: steal, kill, and destroy. I was selling big-time drugs with big-time people, making $10,000 for them and $10,000 for me a week. Then I started doing drugs again. Still on parole, I tested dirty and ended up doing an eighteen- month violation that caused my thinking to shift just a little bit.

Upon my release, I decided I was not ever going to go back to jail. I got a job as a forklift driver for Orchard Supply Hardware. This is where I was introduced to angel dust, an elephant tranquilizer. I was smoking it daily, even at work. I do not know how I was able to maintain a job under the influence of angel dust, but I did.

From there I started a new job as a driver. I was delivering alcohol beverages for a private company. I would leave San Jose early in the mornings and drive to San Francisco. I would deliver all over the Bay Area. I even took it on myself to make me some extra cash by taking extra cases from the warehouse and selling for my own personal habits. One thing about an addict, they have to have a hustle one way or the other, so once I got another job, me and my wife moved down from San Jose to Sacramento.

I even started another job after that, driving for United Cerebral Palsy, a bus company picking up and dropping off children and people with disabilities at school. I was still on drugs, so I got to say it was God. I do believe I have been having a spiritual connection with him all my life. I have no other reason for my still being alive today.

I didn't know at the time, I was covering up a lot of the pain of low self- esteem, consequences of not living right or even being dysfunctional from childhood due to failure of properly being developed in the eyes of God himself or what my eyes was laid on; my heart and mind just couldn't understand. I don't know what the issue was at that time, but I do know I was a functioning addict who was able to keep a job, and with all them jobs, there was a hustle for me to maintain my addiction.

Due to the fact that I continued in my addiction, I lost my wife, but because I did keep a job and the majority of them were driving, I was able to entangle with plenty of people of all sorts, and most of them were women. One of the jobs I had gotten was driving clients to and from their appointments. There was this one lady who I used to pick up for dialyses, and she had taken a liking to me; she wanted me to meet her daughter. I said, "Sure, I will meet your daughter."

I met her daughter, and we became close. We stayed in a relationship for a long time, seven whole years.

The Door through the Demonic Tunnel

At one time in my life while I was still getting high and hanging out in the world, me and some associates that I would get high with, we went through a tunnel where it was scary for me but normal for them.

They thought of this tunnel as a normal safe place to get high. My experience going through that tunnel was like going inside the devil's den, and to my surprise, that was the name of the tunnel. It was written as clear as day, "the devil's den," not one time but several times, all over the walls everywhere. I felt like I took a trip to hell. Something was pulling on me like a hand on my shoulder, pulling me back. I felt demonic spirits all over me. That is one day I ran for my life, as if "Where is it? Where? Help me Lord!" Everyone else was relaxed as relaxed could be, just getting high, not worrying about nothing and nobody. I know God is real, but I know the devil is real also. I experienced him so many times in my life trying to kill me, just so I wouldn't arrive where I am today.

At that time, I felt like the patient of the devil mentioned in the book *Screwtape Letters* by C. S. Lewis. Screwtape plays the role of the devil who sends his nephew Wormwood, instructing him on how to best tempt his patient (a wayward soul on earth), and I was the patient.

I've had numerous times of encounters with the devil. He didn't want to let me go, and today I can look back and know why. Some of these encounters are so deep that they had become unbelievable even to me, but they are true. They did happen; they are real. Satan does come to steal, kill, and destroy.

Still being in the world, living in the darkness only Satan himelf can produce, God had a call for me to come out, but I never knew at that time; all I knew was I was experiencing some weird moments of life.

One day I'm getting high, another day, I'm running from demons, and then all of a sudden I am witnessing to drug addicts coming to smoke crack with me.

Here it is, another day and another time, one of my lady friends coming over, and there it is, a friend of hers with an ounce of cocaine. The devil didn't want to shake me. Yes, I was still in a backsliding state of mind. I did accept Jesus as my personal Savior but not as Lord of my life, not yet anyway. But Jesus was always there for me.

We started getting high, I started to believe he (the young man) wanted to kill me, or either a strong illusion came over me from using the crack cocaine. It does cause one to hallucinate, but to put my mind back in the right perspective, it was God who spoke to my heart to keep me alive. I heard God tell me to ask him if he loves Jesus. I asked him, and his vocal reply was deep and solid as he spoke these words to me, "I come to kill, steal, and destroy. You are lucky, your father has you now." They both got up and left my house.

The very next day, I went to talk to the lady who bought this guy to my house, and her whole house was empty and boarded up. After that night, I never saw her again. Another prime example of the enemy coming in to kill, steal, and destroy. When you're dealing in the world where Satan is the prince of the world, it's easy to lose, lose everything, and possibly never get it back. The world is dark; you can't see where you going or who and what you are falling into. This is how he operates. He's dirty, jealous, and envious of you anyway just because he was rejected by the greatest King to live forever—Jesus Christ, that is. He was rejected because he refused to obey our Father in heaven. So what does he do? He turns the lights off on you and makes you look stupid with your own thoughts and decisions.

"The Enemy comes to steal, Kill and Destroy. but Jesus came so we may have life and have it more abundantly" (John 10:10).

Be careful, he's after your family.

Then I asked God what the meaning of "steal, kill, and destroy" was. He put it in my spirit like this, "The devil steals our joy, kills our soul, and destroys our relationship." That is his whole purpose of being here. He wants to destroy my relationships with the people I love and them who love me.

I was still on parole. I ended up getting a violation for using drugs still. I had to take urine tests so that my parole officer could see if I was still using drugs. One of the stipulations was that I get out of prison and stay free of drugs. That was not happening for me. I didn't understand why then like I do today. God has always been there for me even though the system was cracked. They released me and just told me what I needed to do and what I needed not to do, and drugs was one of them. But God, he had purpose for me, and I just didn't know at that time what my purpose was.

I remember one early morning, about 6:00 a.m., I was sitting on my bed waiting on transportation from one jail to another. I stayed in an open dorm– type of living where the inmates weren't considered dangerous and can freely communicate with one another. I believe at that time, it was about sixteen men to a dorm. I'd decided to read my Bible when an older man came passing by and asked me first how I was doing and then second what I was doing before I could answer, "Fine." Then I said to him, "Just reading my Bible." As he continued to stride on by, he said for me not to worry, I was going back to heaven. I responded, "Okay," not really paying him any attention in the first place, but I guess my worried face was on that day. I read on a little bit more and then all of a sudden, a question came up in my mind for him. I jumped up to go and look for him, but he was gone. I never saw him again.

God Has Angels Watching over Us

Even in jail God has angels watching over you, and that was one of his angels confirming the fact that God was taking care of me even when I didn't know it. Eventually I was released again, only this time, I had to analyze for myself what the parole dos and don'ts really meant.

"Blessed is the one who gains understanding" (Proverbs 3:13).

I went to this church program called the Overcomers for Men. There were fifteen other men, including myself, which totaled sixteen of us. We were the first to start the program. It was a very good Bible teaching program. We had classes three to four times a day. I was still lost and confused. It seemed that I wasn't getting anything out of the program, and all the time, God was preparing me for greatness. I remember playing the quiz games, which were questions out of the Bible. I couldn't understand some and didn't know the answers to the other ones. I began to pray and ask God to give me a spirit of discernment.

In my mind, the spirit of discernment meant knowing all the bad spirits that was around me or inside of people. I also prayed for God to make me a mighty soul winner for his kingdom (winning souls to God is wise) so I would know exactly what to say when the men went out on the streets to win souls back to Christ.

Every time we went out, I would know exactly what to say to save a soul through my testimony. On that one particular day, I set a record of winning forty men back to Christ through the leading of the Holy Spirit. I didn't know at the time winning souls will upset the devil. I didn't know I was boldly going in the enemy's camp to snatch everything God had planned for my life. I was naive. "Zeal without knowledge" is what the Bible calls it.

There was a lot of things I did not know coming in the kingdom, but knowing God existed was not one of them. I knew he was real. Alone my life path, it was him who made sure of that with various signs and wonders, keeping me alive, allowing me chance after chance to be cleansed, and opportunity after opportunity to try again. He would show me his love for me the way no one else could. I didn't know anything about the battlefield or spiritual warfare, and I believe that is why I slipped again and again. Every time, he picked me up like a real father would do for his son. here again, opportunity came for me to be free of drugs, I said again as in so many other times, the enemy shows up inside a female, at the men program I was at, I had the opportunity to watch the house. It was a job, security work, from twelve midnight till morning a couple of nights a week. This was a twelve-month program that became a six-week program to me because I didn't complete it.

It was another one of those bad decisions I made on my own because again, I didn't know.

The reason I was not able to complete the program is because another demonic spirit came, and when it came, it came as a sexual, immoral spirit through a woman. Of course I had known her for a long time. The few nights I was on duty, I would have her come into the van with me so that we can become sexually active. *Boom!* Backsliding again into the sheets of sex. Like psalmist Juanita Bynum says, "Right back in the sheets again." That's real. It was another one of those bad decisions I made on my own because again, I didn't know, which caused me to hit on a point of studying your Bible and not just reading it. Everything God's Word says is real from loving him with your whole heart, which is taught throughout the *whole* Bible, to teaching your hands how to war and your fingers to fight (Psalm 144:1; KJV).

We have to know how to fight coming in the kingdom of God because demons are real, and they travel through people, mostly the ones closest to you. Everyone has a soul, and it can be a vehicle for Satan, or it can become a vessel for God to move through with the Holy Spirit in Jesus Christ of Nazareth's name.

"The fruit of the righteous is a tree of life; and he that winneth souls is wise" (Proverbs 11:30).

I didn't choose myself for the kingdom business; it was already established before I even reached this earth.

Jerimiah 29:11 says, "I know the plans I have for you says the Lord, thoughts of peace and not of evil, to give you an expected end."

He gave me exactly what I asked for the same way he gave Solomon what he asked for. I asked to be able to discern demons in order to bring souls back to Christ. But apparently I didn't know how to discern when God sent me to the program, and I'm believing in my heart right now that every demonic encounter that God allowed to come my way was an empowerment to answer my prayer of becoming the mighty man of God that he personally ordained me to be. Besides, he gives us what we ought to pray for. Sometimes we forget what we pray for, but God doesn't.

Pray for anything according to his will, and it shall be done for you.

In the midst of God spinning me into a new person, I kept trying to stay in a world of sin. I chose to call that woman to the van those nights when I was going through trials and tribulations. I still had a desire to become whole, but because God wanted me to see that lustful spirit operating in me and where he was taking me, I couldn't take that Spirit. The lady even said I could come and live with her. It wasn't her, she wasn't on drugs, it was me. I was on drugs. She is living in Denver, Colorado, doing really well for herself. She wanted me to go with her so we can start a new beginning, but God said no. Through my drug addiction, I'm right where he wants me to be.

Even in my struggle to pursue wholeness, even in my weakness for him to become my strength, and even with every backsliding demon encounter experience, God had positioned me every time because that is what I prayed for, so don't be careful to pray, just pray. He will answer in his own timing so correctly, you have to know it is him. There is no way of getting around the fact that God is on his throne.

Opening Demonic Doors of Death

I was just a lost soul, not knowing which way to go, or even what to do next step.

I remember getting high at my mother's house. I would go to the bathroom and hit the pipe. It seemed like every time I would hit the pipe, the lights in the bathroom will flicker off and on. I don't know if this was actually happening in my head or if the lights really were going on and off, but I do believe, as I look back on those moments, that every time I went there to smoke the crack cocaine, I was opening up doors to death.

I was opening doors for demonic forces, and I didn't know.

Later on, my brother died inside the house, and one year later, my mother passed away.

I have to talk about how I was being delivered from drugs. I started to live inside my mother's house after she had passed away. I was living there, and one of my sisters was living there with me. I was in the back room inside my mother's house at the time. I was sleep. I woke up to pain. I actually witnessed my arm bubbling up. I believe it was the devil. He didn't want to release me to the Holy Spirit.

That drug spirit had lived in my body for so long, it didn't want to depart from me, but God, he was not having it anymore, so the Holy Spirit came and kicked those demons out. I witnessed the fight in my arms bubbling up and down. My God delivered me that night. I had become free of drugs once again, although it was painful. It reminded me of a quote, "No pain, no gain." It was more difficult for me this time because I relapsed and backslid at the same time, and seven more demons came inside my temple of God. I didn't know in order to live in the kingdom of God, I had to keep my temple full of the Word and prayer, talking to God all the way through and about my life. I had to have a Shepherd; I was a lost sheep. God is one above all, and we have to be balanced and lined up to his Word in order to gain stability and stay saved.

I truly believe drugs is a generation curse in my family or just a familiar spirit.

Opening the Door to a Friend

I opened my front door to a friend who was at the lowest point of his life. He was like a brother to me, and while he was living with me, he opened the front door of the house unknowingly to the spiritual battles that was taking place in my life at this particular time and through the doors which they would occur.

While I was away from the house one day, he allowed a lady friend of mine to come inside the house. He was not aware of her intentions, and she was not aware of the devil and his intentions or his way to kill, steal, and destroy. She said she needed to use the bathroom. She actually lied to him and said I told her that was okay. She went inside the bathroom to hit some drugs and left the house in a hurry. I never found out about this until later.

I do believe by her coming inside the house to hit them drugs, she allowed a demonic spirit to enter into the house. By this time, I was already saved, sanctified, and set free. That night when I went to bed, about 2:00 a.m., I was attacked, straddled by a demon on the bed. It was heavy. It applied spiritual pain as well, pain I would probably relate to that of a woman in labor. It acted as if it didn't want to move off me. It took about four to five minutes of me crying out to God for that demon to loosen his grip on me, and all because I called on the name of Jesus. I actually cried and cried out loud so that the Lord can help me. Then I found out later when I saw the lady that hit the pipe in the bathroom at my house, she said that the devil forced her to do it so that I can be attached by the demons.

Leroy Brownlow wrote in his devotional book titled *Today Is Mine*, "Age can bud again, it takes years to grow an oak—and a man. Both lumber and brains season with time. Deep rivers had had the flow of many waters, and deep minds have had the passing of many thoughts."

Most of the great men distinguished themselves after fifty. Distinction requires more than impulsive actions, guided movements; more than high speed, directions.

The university of hard knocks has its lessons; they are hard but effective. The price of getting wiser is getting older, plus getting a few bumps and bruises. Years should teach, and if one is an apt student, they will.

"And now in age I bud again" (George Herbert).

"I said, Days should speak, and multitude of years should teach wisdom" (Job 32:7).

Demonic Door Straight to the Devil

This is about another encounter with the devil.

I remember getting high with some people in my apartment, and they would say to me, "Did you see that snake?" They were so scared.

I believed them. I just didn't see what they saw. People came to my house all the time to smoke crack, and they will always go inside the bathroom to smoke. They will stay inside the bathroom for a long time, pretty much until I tell them to come out. While they were in there, I will always hear noise, as if they were talking to someone.

Every time they hit the pipe, demonic doors would open. The devil would always be on them. It was like Satan had a personal interview with me. Every time they came out of the bathroom, their demeanor was different. At this particular time, I was so far gone out there. I was high as I don't know and wanted to continue to get high. Even now I was feeling these demonic spirits on me, it didn't stop me. I continued to get high. You would think that a person wanted to put the pipe down and run for their life, meeting the devil in person, but I didn't run. I stayed, and so did they. I kept opening the door for the devil every time he knocked on the door.

I was feeling those demonic encounters every time I opened the front door, but it seemed like getting high was more important to me. I realize now that I was in some deep bondage so far down, and the only way up was God's outstretched hand. I remember having a dream, and inside this dream, I could look down this tunnel and see a little light, and the light looked like it was about to go out. If that light would have gone out, it would have been pitch dark. I woke up interpreting the dream as almost losing my soul to the devil, and that little light that didn't go out was the light of God in my spirit, which actually saved my life.

When I woke up, I had scratches on my back. First thing came to my mind was the devil scratched me up trying to pull me down to hell. I was already spiritually bankrupt, but God, he raised me up the same as he did Lazarus when he was dead. He call him, Lazarus, come forward.

Then Jesus said in a loud voice and said, "Lazarus, come forth" (John 11:43).

That little light I saw was the calling of God. He had a plan for me. I had to live for his purpose to be filled inside my life.

Now I know my purpose in God and every demonic experience I had was for me to know how to discern demons in other people and cast them out instead of having pity for that person, interfering in the good works of the Lord in people's lives. I love the Lord for keeping me, and if you are reading this book, it is simply because you want God to do the same for you. I know and pray that he will.

The death of my brother came right after the trial of me being scattered on my bed from the release of demons that was coming from the bathroom. It is true, when you open the door for sin to come in, death will take its place one way or another. It could be spiritual, natural, or even mental, but the demons will come through the doors that we open. My brother was fifty-four years old, and he died of a heart attack. It really hurt my mother, and she passed away a year later. That really hurt me and a lot of other family members. I didn't know how to process that pain. It was pain on top of pain.

I moved into my mother's house after she died. Back in the bathroom I go, hitting the pipe harder and harder, trying to drown the pain by inhaling cocaine that went straight to my head so quick and stayed in my head. I was thinking the thoughts running rapidly in my head would just fade away. It only made me get more and more to smoke in order for me not to think about the death of my brother and mother, but it wasn't working. Every time I took a hit of the pipe inside the bathroom at my mother's house, the lights would flip on and off, and I know I was opening demonic doors, but I didn't care, and that made everything get worse.

I couldn't handle it anymore. The guilt and shame I had to carry was getting too heavy. The shame of knowing my mother and brother passed in this house and guilt was eating my soul up. The drugs couldn't take the pain away. I broke down and asked God again for forgiveness and to come into my heart a little later when I just couldn't do it anymore. I gave up drugs through the mercy and grace of God. He saved my life. I could have been dead and gone, but God didn't let me go. He had a plan for me to live and decree that he is Lord. He delivered me from drugs and everything else that was not pleasing to him. He set me free. My testimony is him. I couldn't do it on my own.

So after giving my life back to God, the battles began; they were some serious battles. I remember sleeping in the back room of my mother's house. I was awakened by pain in my arms.

My arms started to bubble up; it was a battle in my arms.

It was very painful for me, and when I looked at my arms, they were bubbling up, and, yes, it was a very fearful moment for me. I didn't know exactly what was going on. I could see the battle and feel the pain. Those drug demons did not want to release me. My body was their home. I had bought seven stronger demons to join the ones that was there already, and they were fighting in my arm, trying to stay. I was clean, no drugs. Sometimes when we are on drugs, we can see these demonic spirits really well. Some people may think it is hallucination, but no, it is real. I have been clean long enough and good enough for God to allow the Holy Spirit to show up and deliver me from the strong hold of drugs.

I was set free and delivered from myself, I say *myself* because it was me who was on drugs, and all the laws of the drug war was perfected in me, from robberies to selling drugs and all the in-betweens. Experiencing this freedom from the bondage of drugs, I became a servant for the Most High to dwell in me. I had developed a zeal that most people get in the beginning of their salvation. God had laid in my spirit to win souls for him. When you experience the freedom of what God is able to do through his glory, you become really appreciative of what is happening in your life and the manifestation of God's glory comes into effect, and it causes you to be willing and obedient.

I couldn't understand the Bible at that time, or shall I say God had not open his Word up yet for me to understand it. Unless the Lord does it, It will not happen. I prayed and asked God to at least allow me to go and win souls for his glory, also to allow me to have discernment of the demons that are in people. Be careful what you pray for. He might not answer you right then and there, but he will answer. He is an on-time God, and he did answer my prayer. I also prayed for God to give me more faith than Abraham, so I was tested big time in my faith. So be careful what you pray for.

So I would ride my bike every day Monday through Fridays daily except for the weekends, for a whole year witnessing for the Lord, winning three to seven souls daily. The Spirit of God was really working in me at that time.

When God saves you from a life of sin, there is a zeal that consumes you, and all you want to do is run and tell the world about the love of God and how God has bought you out of darkness and into his marvelous light. I haven't even been saved long enough to get the education I needed inside the body of Christ.

Proverbs 19:2 tells us, "It is dangerous to have zeal without knowledge, and the one who act hastily makes poor choices."

Now I can see I don't have to keep bumping into Satan and his desires.

God has a life for me and also life for you, my reader.

I remember one encounter. I was witnessing and ran upon a man who had a hood over his head. His head was hanging down. I went to shake his hand. When he looked up at me, darkness covered him, and he scared me for a second or two. I went to ask him about Jesus. He tried to speak, but he could not, he just murmured. The demonic spirit had such a hold on him. He was so bond, he couldn't call out to Jesus. When I got to the house, I took off my clothing and saw a big black mark on my arm that caused me to fear. One of the best ways for the enemy to come in is through fear.

You have either fear or faith. Faith is of God, and fear is of the devil. I operate in faith. I believe God can move mountains, so when I saw the big of black mark on my arm, I was able to lay my other hand on my arm and pray for God's healing, and behold, the next day my arm was heal. I thank the Lord once again.

God is a healer, and he does for us what we cannot do for yourself. As I continued on, I remember while I was out witnessing, I ran into a couple of females. And surely females are one of my weaknesses. Before I can start to witness to them, they seduced me sexually by saying to me what they would do to me sexually, and all of a sudden, everything God had sent me to do disappeared until the three 6's appeal.

They convinced me to go into the store to get a drink. That drink and my excitement was refunded when the man told me the drink totality of $6.66. I then realized that I could not be with them whether they liked it or not, and they didn't like it, but the fear of God came on me so strong. I had to let them go. Praise God all the days of my life for doing for me what I cannot do for myself.

One thing we do have to realize and that is our weaknesses as well as our strengths. It was then I realize that God is our strength even in our weaknesses,

"Let the weak say I am strong" (Joel 3:10; NKJV).

There will be many spiritual battles for me with women.

So this is another one of my spiritual battles with a woman but in a different matter. I guess it all comes with the daily training with my hands, for God is my teacher.

I had so many lady friends, and that can tell you a lot about me when I was in the world unsaved. I was home just relaxing one day, and all of a sudden the phone rang, and there she was again, only this time it was ministry, warfare, something I was not aware of or even expecting.

It was a warm nice day, the kind of day in Sacramento, California, when you stayed in the house. I answered, and to my surprise, it was a friend I had known for the last five years wanting me to come to her house, claiming there was some demons inside her house and she was scared to go home. She actually wanted me to come and pray them demons out of her house. This was shocking to me because I have never done this before. I even had to call another one of my women friends to ask her what I should do in a situation like this.

Her advice was, "Take someone with you and pray before going in there." I then explained to her I didn't know anyone, so she prayed on the phone with me, gave me some instructions on how to go inside the house and pray the demons out so that the woman can then take access of her own house again. Everything went well, and that is what happened. The woman had become comfortable in her own house.

Then one day, the pastor of my church, Pastor Carter, at Faithland Missionary Baptist Church in Sacramento, California, asked me if I could go with one of the members of the church and pray over his family and their house as well. I said yes. I was very surprised that God worked through the pastor to help build my faith, and I never told the pastor what I did at my lady friend's house when she asked me to come over and pray those evil spirits out their house. God is an all-knowing God.

"For we do not wrestle against flesh and blood, but against principalities, against powers, against the rulers of the darkness of this age, [c] against spiritual hosts of wickedness in the heavenly places" (Ephesians 6:12).

The Holy Spirit used me again to do just that, bind every demon and evil spirit that was in that place. Then two weeks later, he called me again to do the same thing inside another family's house, and of course, my answer was yes. Lord, send me where you want me to go.

The brother who called and depended on me to go with him was James. We arrived at the house, and there it is, I started using this holy oil around the door post of this family's home to bless it. I noticed one of the brothers of this family really trying to get away. I was blessing the inside of the house when I noticed him. I had already anointed the family members, but the family member would not let me come near him with the holy oil. When talking to him, I noticed a demonic spirit inside of him talking back to me. He was actually quoting Scripture, the Word of God to me. (That reminded me of the devil tempting God when he had to be tested by the devil before he could make the next step.)

But God was not late in showing up for me and with me, working right alongside me like he does all of us when he sends us out on an assignment. God spoke to me and told me to "use your sword, the Word of God" to shut him up, and I did. When on assignments for God, we have to do and listen to every small whisper even when it is noisy. The man became so afraid, he left the house.

But when that mission was over, the only thing that kept stirring in my brain was, *How did my brother at the church know my gift?* I know God said that my gifts will make room for me, and they did speedily. They didn't know about the other house I went to. All I can say is "Thank you, God."

I would love to thank my wife lajuana Washington for being my backbone, and my friend in Christ Jesus Lamar for keeping me lifted by saying, "You just keep pressing toward the higher mark." I would first give glory to my God who is in heaven for allowing the Holy Spirit to speak to me and through me as I had the opportunity to witness over five thousand souls won unto the kingdom of God. Hallelujah, hallelujah, and hallelujah. Amen.

Author's Note:

I'm pretty much saying that, in life, there are doors in everything we do. When I was witnessing for the Lord Jesus, I was the first door to God, bringing people to Christ, the salvation door. Then, next door, someone would water the seed I planted through the Holy Spirit. And finally, the increased door that came by God alone.

Let's talk about how I had the opportunity to witness to so many people. It started when I was in the overcoming home in Sacramento, California, for a one-year program for men. We would go out to witness and I really liked it—just knowing I was doing something good made me feel content. After the overcoming program, I moved to my mother's house. The spirit guided me in a sense to get up every morning and ride my bike to win souls for the Lord. I did it for a year, averaging five to seven souls daily. Additionally, my church also went out every month in Sacramento to witness for the Lord.

I later moved to San Francisco to stay with my grandmother, where I joined her church. I became the outreach minister, and we went out monthly to witness. We averaged about 30 souls a month, 73 being the biggest soul-winning day, a truly blessed day, especially in the tenderloins in San Francisco.

However, the devil found some old tickets back in Sacramento. I had to go to court and they gave me six months for some old tickets—train tickets mostly. While in jail, I got a job in the clothing room where they either get released or come in to do some time. That was my morning job for the natural world. My spiritual job came in the evening. The officers would let me read the daily word every night, and before doing so, I would offer salvation to the inmates. The participants averaged between 20-30 men daily for six months.

To this day, the Holy Spirit still speaks to me and through me as I witness for the Lord Jesus Christ.

About the Author

Mr. Lavance Washington is an ordained deacon. He was ordained on July 16, 2017. He has been a Christian most of his life but didn't get filled with the Holy Ghost until the year 2012. Since then, he's been on fire for the Lord Jesus Christ. His passion is winning souls for the Lord Jesus Christ. He loves bike riding and watching the sun set on the shore by the beach. He has two beautiful children; both are girls, and they are grown now. He has one grandchild. His greatest accomplishment is becoming an ordained deacon. It's truly a blessing from God Almighty to serve him and his saints. Hallelujah. Glory to God. Amen, amen, and amen.

www.ingramcontent.com/pod-product-compliance
Lightning Source LLC
Chambersburg PA
CBHW031237120626
46545CB00003B/1160